So will I sing the praises
of Your name forever,
fulfilling my vows
day by day.
                    Psalm 61:9

The intent and
purpose of this volume is to
give you faith, hope and inspira-
tion. Hopefully it will help bring peace
and tranquility into your life. May it be a
reminder of God's love, guidance
and His many blessings.

Our publications help to support our work
for needy children in over 120 countries
around the world. Through our
programs, thousands of children are
fed, clothed, educated, sheltered
and given the opportunity to
live decent lives.

Salesian Missions wishes to extend special thanks and gratitude to our
generous poet friends and to the publishers who have given us permission t
reprint material included in this book. Every effort has been made to give
proper acknowledgments. Any omissions or errors are deeply regretted, and
the publisher, upon notification, will be pleased to make the necessary
corrections in subsequent editions.

First Edition Printed in the U.S.A. by Concord Litho Group, Concord, New
Hampshire 03301.

Sing
His Praises
from the
Salesian Collection

Compiled and edited by
Jennifer Grimaldi

Illustrated by
Dale Begley, Russell Bushée,
Frank Massa, Maureen McCarthy,
Paul Scully and Robert Van Steinburg

Contents

Petals of Gold..............................6

Welcome May 7

Announcing, "It Is Spring".........8

The Sunflowers.........................10

Strengthen Me 11

April's Reign 12

Trust in the Lord 14

There Are Moments 15

On a Summer Day 17

God Is Real 18

God Provides 19

The Story of My Life...............20

The Wonder of His Works 22

The Song of Autumn 23

Autumn 24

God's Way of Telling Us..........26

Peace Is.....................................27

At Eventide 28

Jesus Waits 29

Winter Wonderment 30

Faith 32

Tomorrow May Be Too Late ..33

Life's Recipe 35

Seeds of Faith..........................36

Start With a Joyful Heart 38

I Can 39

I Have Seen My Savior............40

Silent Symphony 42

Look Beyond.............................43

My Chosen Companion..........44

Life's Moments.........................46

He Will See Us Through 47

Window Sightings 48

God Bless the Children 49

An Autumn Tapestry 50

Autumn Assurance..................51

Changing Scenes 52

God's Wonders 54

God's Golden Autumn
    Treasures 55

Autumn Blessings 56

Strengthen Me, Lord 58

Know That God Is
    Beside You 59

His Tender Love 60

Some Small Way 62

The Silent Days 63

Winter Ballet............................64

Springtime Robins...................66

Heartfelt Words of Praise 67

When Winter Turns
  to Spring 68
Jesus, I Feel Your Peace...........70
Born Anew 71
Summertime.........................72
August Song 73
Listening to the Quiet 74
My Little Corner 75
The Earth Sings Forth 76
Lord, Lead Me 78
Footsteps by the Seashore 79
The Last Days of Summer 80
I'm Always Chasing
  Rainbows 82
Autumn 83
Fall Is in the Air 84
I Shall Not Want.....................86
My Overseer and Guide..........87
Autumntime 88
Never Alone 91
When Winter Comes!.............92
God's Blessings 94
Bits of Joy 95
Winter Nighttime Wonder......96
Spring Beauties 98

Throughout the Day................99
Each Spring Is New 100
Gratitude...............................102
My Riches 103
On a Golden
  Summer's Day.................. 104
Make a Joyful Noise 106
Bridges of Understanding 107
Those Hazy Days of Summer 108
God Is Everything I Need 110
A Rose 111
For All Tomorrows 112
Have You?..............................114
His Blessings All
  Around Us 115
The Voice of God 116
God Is Everywhere 118
Comfort 119
At Harvest Time.....................120
A Prayer.................................122
Trust 123
Love, Perfect Love 124
The Snow 126
When There Is Love 127
A Moment in Time 128

Petals of Gold

Raindrops of silver bring petals of gold
When Spring's crimson skies vanquish the cold
As flowers burst forth from Winter's cold grave
To bask in the sun, to dance and to wave.
All earth's a garden beneath sunny skies
For every sunrise brings a brand-new surprise.
Each day's a treasure, a sight to behold,
When God writes "I love you" on petals of gold.

Clay Harrison

Welcome May

Welcome May, sweet child of Spring,
Such a joyous happening.
Tulips lend us wondrous charms
Tucked within your loving arms.
Skies of blue are smiling down,
Blessing country lane and town.

Welcome May, with golden sun,
Moments filled with happy fun.
Hush of morning just at dawn,
Sunset when the day is gone.
New beginnings all our own,
Dreams to dream when we're alone.

Springtime lends a blessing real
Bringing precious thoughts ideal.
Gentle breezes, cooling rain,
Nature comes to life again.
Wildflowers bloom along the way,
All the world now welcomes May.

Garnett Ann Schultz

Announcing, "It Is Spring"

'Tis the season of the year
To set aside all care,
Time to enjoy the beauty
Around you everywhere.

Thrill to the coming of the dawn
In the early morning light,
Then later on at eventide,
Rest in the gentle night.

Seeds all planted in a row
Begin to show their heads,
Dandelions appear too soon
In well-trimmed garden beds.

Lawns are mowed with loving care.
In manicured rows of flowers,
To pull the weeds as they appear
Takes patience and long hours.

Observe the nesting of the birds,
The mating songs they sing,
Trills and warbles fill the air
Announcing, "It is Spring."

Ruth Moyer Gilmour

The Sunflowers

In the stillness of the morning
When the sunshine grips the day
And the shadows of the nighttime
Have quietly slipped away,
They raise their smiling faces,
As yellow as the sun,
As if to say to all the world,
"Good morning, everyone."

Throughout the brightness of the day,
They lift their faces high,
They follow the sun's bright light
As it moves through the sky.
Oh, may we, like the sunflowers,
Look to the Lord each day,
For He puts the sunshine in our hearts
When we follow in His way.

Loise Pinkerton Fritz

Strengthen Me...

Strengthen me, oh precious Lord;
My life I give to Thee;
Release me from all pain and fear,
And set my spirit free...

Strengthen me, oh precious Lord;
Fill me with blessed hope;
I look to Thee for love and peace;
Oh, come and help me cope...

Strengthen me, oh precious Lord;
Uplift my doubting soul;
Renew my faith and trust in Thee
That I may reach my goal...

Hope C. Oberhelman

Cast all your worries upon Him
because He cares for you.
1 Peter 5:7

April's Reign

Pink-white blossoms on the trees,
Petaled fragrance fills the breeze,
Robin redbreast sings along
With the tumbling brooklet's song.
Daffodils raise frilly heads
From their golden flowerbeds;
And the tulip cups unfold
Wondrous colors to behold.
Pussy willows soft and gray
On their switches gently sway.

Verdant carpets deck the hills,
Sunbeams dance on mountain rills.
Daisies white dot meadows green
And above this charming scene,
There's a canopy of blue,
Fluffy cloudlets stealing through.
All the earth is bright and fair,
April's reigning everywhere;
Stretching far as eye can see
Is Spring in all her finery!

Beverly J. Anderson

Splendor and majesty go before Him;
praise and joy are in His holy place.
1 Chronicles 16:27

Trust in the Lord

When you feel you've arrived
At the end of your rope,
Do not despair
Because there is hope.
Just ask our Lord
Who is all kind and good,
For your every word
Will be understood.
He is always listening
And will answer your need.
Have faith and trust
In the Lord indeed.

Jo March

There Are Moments

There are moments given me
When I feel so full of You,
And Your presence overwhelms me,
...Dearest Lord, I never knew
Loving You could be like this,
Why did You wait so long
To show me how to please You
'Til the years were almost gone?

Did You think I was not ready
To accept You as You are?
That I was not strong enough
To follow You so far?
If so, why did You let me
Get close enough to see
Your longing and Your hunger,
And Your burning love for me?

So now I cannot leave You,
For I would cease to be.
Do what You will with me, my Lord,
...For all eternity.
And all the wonder that is You
Will be my treasure when,
Close to Your heart, I live these moments
...Over and again!

Grace E. Easley

On a Summer Day

There's a softness on a Summer day
That comes no other time;
A softness on the azure sky
That makes our day sublime.

There's a softness in the sunbeams
And in the gentle rain
As it washes flower faces
And makes them bright again.

There's a softness on the distant hills,
A softness in the green
That bids us come and rest awhile
From out life's busy scene.

There's a softness in the meadow
With pretty daisies blessed;
And in the mother robin's song,
Wee babies in the nest.

There's a softness on the Summer breeze,
A softness in the touch.
On a Summer day God whispers,
"I love you very much."

Kay Hoffman

God Is Real

God is as real as a Summer breeze,
For He can be found on the wind.
Softly comforting fingers of love
Move lightly over my skin.

I know He is there, I hear His sweet voice
Whispering hope to me,
Telling me all will be well with my soul
Because He wants it to be.

Patiently now, I stand here in awe
Of God's infallible plan
To always be near and care for me here,
And to never let go of my hand.

Myrtle Lee Johnson

God Provides

I choose not to share my troubles,
Nor the scars down deep inside;
But I've found through all adversity
God always does provide.

When our pathway seems the darkest
And life's storms are all about,
We've used all our resources
And it seems there's no way out;
That's when He sends a miracle –
Moves mountains – calms the sea,
But oftentimes the miracle
Is worked inside of me.

He gives us strength for every need,
Gives joy in times of sorrow,
And I know with deep assurance
He'll be there for me tomorrow.

Martha Mastin

*Then, taking along some of the fruit
of the land, they brought it down to
us and reported, "The land which
the Lord, our God, gives us is good."*
Deuteronomy 1:25

19

The Story of My Life

Eagerly and joyously
I greet my days and nights.
I think of them as pages
In a storybook I write.

My Father's grand and glorious world,
The beauties I behold
Make a perfect setting
As my life unfolds.

Page by page and day by day,
My life's events engage.
I hold to what is good and true
As I turn each page.

The theme of my life's story
Is to learn and do, each day,
The will of my Creator,
In God's own perfect way.

I feel God's harmony and peace
Even in days of strife.
I'm joyously developing
The story of my life!

Micky Meyer Mathewson

The Wonder of His Works

Sometimes I'm caught in wonder
Seeing the works of God's own hands.
I'm grateful for the beauty
He bestowed upon our land.

The mountains high and valleys deep
And rivers that murmur sweet songs
Are all a part of the beauty
In a world to which I belong.

I love to feel the gentle breeze
That whispers through the trees,
And sit upon the sandy shore
To watch the sun set o'er the sea.

Oh yes, I'm thankful for my God
Who loves us beyond compare.
He placed a rainbow in the sky
To remind us He is always there.

Shirley Hile Powell

The Song of Autumn

The crisp and cool October winds
Sing softly through the trees
That dance the dance of ages past
In tune to Autumn's breeze.

They shed their gold and scarlet crowns
Beneath the skies of blue
As restless winds now touched with frost
Come briskly blowing through.

Long, icy fingers hush the lake
And lace the window glass,
Where green fields sleep in silence as
The days of Summer pass.

The Autumn winds that sing their songs
Will soon hear Winter's call,
When evergreens like mountains stand
In cold white snows that fall!

Kate Watkins Furman

*To everything there is a season,
and a time to every purpose.*
Ecclesiastes 3:1

Autumn

The golden leaves of Autumn
Are rustling in the trees,
Murmuring a melody
Of Autumn memories.

Past glories of the springtime
When leaves were fair and green,
And birds intent on building nests
Urged by God, unseen…

Are whispered in the rustling;
A dreaming of the past
When days could seem to never end,
But it could never last.

Now the glory days are here.
Each leaf does God imbue
With power to become much more
And to reflect Him, too.

Oh, may our lives resplendent be
With golden deeds well done...
Guided by the hand of God
And blessed by His dear Son.

Margaret Peterson

The Lord bless you and keep you!
The Lord let His face shine upon you,
and be gracious to you! The Lord look
upon you kindly and give you peace!
Numbers 6:24-26

God's Way of Telling Us

I wonder why just one limb
Starts coloring on a tree,
And why the dogwood finds itself
With just one bright red leaf.
I wonder why the ears of corn
Hang low upon the stalks,
And why, at every turn of eye,
There are paintings by Jack Frost.

I wonder why the birds fly south
In migratory form,
And why the sumac by the streams
With red plumes are adorned.
I wonder why the lady-slippers
Tuck away their shoes…
It's God's own way of telling us
That autumntime's in view.

Loise Pinkerton Fritz

Peace Is

Peace is a sky of heavenly blue,
A rainbow so bright when the storm clouds are through,
One blooming rose in a garden of love,
A million soft stars that shine from above,
A cool April shower that blesses the Spring
And moments of quiet the evening hours bring.

Peace is a hilltop – a tree reaching tall,
The bright sparkling colors that welcome the Fall,
It's blossoms and green leaves that dear Maytime lends,
The laughter of children – the blessing of friends,
A small furry kitten – the boss of our home,
A boy and the puppy he claims as his own.

A million small treasures we hold in our heart,
The faith and believing that hope can impart,
A sunbeam – a raindrop – a snowflake of white,
The moments at dawning – the beauty of night,
A dream we are dreaming – a smile or a kiss,
The soft touch of Nature – we know peace is this.

Garnett Ann Schultz

How varied are Your works, O Lord!
In wisdom You have wrought them all-
the earth is full of Your creatures.
Psalm 104:24

27

At Eventide

When evening shadows cover all,
I put my cares away
And bless the evening, for it brings
Rest from burdens of the day.

My soul springs up at eventide
When menial tasks are done;
And weary hands once more relax
Each setting of the sun.

Though days be long with endless chores,
I thank my God for all;
With prayerful heart, for rest that's ours
When evening shadows fall.

Gene Appleby

Jesus Waits

When life becomes a burden –
Filled with heartaches and despair –
And no human soul will help you
With your need for love and care;
And you cry in quiet corners
And you live with growing fears,
Come to Jesus – for salvation –
And be rescued and endeared.

He awaits with love and mercy
For all hearts that cry alone
And the souls that weep for kindness
For the hurts that life intones.
He will not deny your wishes
If you come to Him in prayer,
And you ask for the salvation
Of His love and holy care.

Michael Dubina

You fixed all the limits of the land;
Summer and Winter You made.
Psalm 74:17

Winter Wonderment

When temperatures are low,
The snow is piling deep,
Some people close up in the house,
Just use the time to sleep.

Not I, I love the splendor,
So I can find no reason
To miss the Winter wonderment
And the creatures of the season.

The birds know who their friends are
As they fly up to our hill.
They know we always welcome them
As we peer out near the sill.

The snowbird and the finches,
The cardinal painted red.
No, Winter is not dismal,
Quite colorful instead.

The deer, the perfect image
Of magnificence and grace.
I see them scamper on the trail,
Then quickly turn to chase.

Just sitting at my window,
I could not ask for more
Except to view it all again
When Winter's at my door.

Nancy Tant

Faith

It's said that faith is confidence
And I believe it's so,
And if we exercise our faith,
It's bound to grow and grow.

Faith is belief that God is real,
Can save and sanctify,
And confidence that daily He
Will all our needs supply.

And faith is knowledge that our God
Will hear us when we pray,
That He knows just what's best for us –
Will lead us day by day.

So let us exercise our faith
And let us always know
That faith is confidence, my friend –
Let's help it grow and grow.

Luther Elvis Albright

Tomorrow
May Be Too Late

Lord let me not grow weary
Of the tasks that lie ahead,
So many things need to be done,
So many hearts to mend.

Let me go that extra mile,
Let me speak that tender word.
No need to say you're sorry
If the words cannot be heard.

Time goes by so very fast,
It's much later than we think.
Do all those good things while you can –
Tomorrow may be too late!

Fern R. Ackerman

*Fill us at daybreak with Your kindness,
that we may shout for joy and
gladness all our days.*
Psalm 90:14

*Y*ou have made known to me
the paths of life; You will fill me
with joy in Your presence.

Acts 2:28

Life's Recipe

A cup full of sunbeams,
A dash of sky blue,
A spoonful of dewdrops,
A rainbow or two,
The soft touch of dawning
To light morning's way,
One bright, glowing sunset
At closing of day.

Blend in a rainbow
Just after the storm,
The flowers of springtime,
A June day that's warm,
The sparkle of Autumn
With leaves colored bright,
A breeze gently blowing,
Some starshine at night.

Mix in a snowflake,
A cloud-step above,
The laughter of children,
A portion of love,
Some prayer and believing,
A heart that is free,
Mix them together,
You've life's recipe.

Garnett Ann Schultz

Seeds of Faith

Use me, Lord, in some small way
To help someone somewhere today.
Help me bear my brother's load
If he should fall upon life's road.
Teach me, Lord, to know Thy ways
That I might serve You all my days.
Fill my heart with love divine;
Impart Thy will and make it mine.

Give me strength when I am weak
And bless the words I choose to speak
That I might glorify Thy name
And minimize my claim to fame.
Fill me, Lord, till I overflow
With seeds of faith where'er I go.
Root them deep within my soul
And may they blossom pure and whole.
Use me, Lord, in some small way
To help someone somewhere today.

Clay Harrison

Start With a Joyful Heart

Start with a joyful heart
For all the happy things
Which come your way
From day to day,
The joy which Nature brings.

Start with a prayerful heart
Which praises as it sings
Songs of glory and of love,
Sounds of a bell that rings.

Start with a hopeful heart,
Look forward to the best
That life doth offer
Now and then,
May you be forever blest.

Start with a grateful heart,
Thanks to our heavenly Lord
For peace and love
And hope and joy,
To never know discord.

Marilyn McNeil de Latour

I Can

I can start my day with laughter,
I can fill it with my song,
Bright'ning every little moment
As the day hours slip along.

I can lift the nighttime shadows,
Make it seem as light as day,
All I need is faith, sincerely,
When I kneel to praise and pray.

I can make my life more useful
When I have a higher goal,
Thinking less of me than others –
Keeping Jesus in my soul.

Rachel Hartnett

I Have Seen My Savior

I have seen my Savior
In springtime's budding trees,
In Summer's flowered hillsides,
In Autumn's swirling breeze.

I have heard His voice distinctly
In the laughter of a child
And sensed His mighty power
When Winter storms run wild.

I have known His precious comfort
In sorrow and in grief.
His loving arms around me
Have strengthened my belief.

Yes, I have seen my Savior
In the fullness of my days.
Because of this I give Him
My worship and my praise.

His visage is reflected
Each morning, fresh and new.
He is always there beside me.
Have you seen your Savior, too?

Jean Conder Soule

Silent Symphony

I saw a glorious symphony
As sunrise filled the skies;
My soul rose up with praising wings
Greeting God in this lovely disguise.

I saw a marvelous symphony
Rippling from cloud to cloud
And felt creation's immensity
As an eternal promise avowed.

I saw a majestic symphony
Of brilliant color unfold
And knew that of God's mercy,
Greater cannot be told.

I saw a silent symphony
Which blessed me without a word –
And I promised to live my life today
As a joy, a love both felt and heard.

Pollyanna Sedziol

Look Beyond

Look beyond your suffering.
Look beyond your fear.
Look beyond your adversity,
And find the Lord so near.

Look beyond the problem.
Look beyond the now.
Look beyond the turmoil,
And before Him humbly bow.

For, in looking beyond and bowing,
You will find your normal sight
Takes on spiritual vision
In God's sustaining light.

Josephine Anne Miller

With your own eyes you
have seen all these great deeds
that the Lord has done.
Deuteronomy 11:7

43

My Chosen Companion

On the highways that we travel –
In our span of life and time –
There are mountains we must conquer;
There are hills that we must climb;
And our choice – at every crossroad –
Must be made with special care,
Lest we choose the road to nowhere
That is always present there.

We must also choose, with prudence,
Who will walk with us each way;
Who will share with us our burdens
And the glories of each day,
For each dawn will bring new journeys
With an end we can't foresee –
And our choice of a companion
Could decide our destiny.

I have chosen One of spirit
Who will walk with me each road –
Never leave me or forsake me
To my struggles or my load –
And His love for me is proven
By two thousand years of time:
I will walk through life with Jesus
And will live by His design.

Michael Dubina

I will instruct you and show you the
way you should walk; I will counsel
you, keeping my eye on you.
Psalm 32:8

Life's Moments

Life's moments form a tapestry,
A truly fine design;
Some threads are dark with pain and grief,
Some bright with joy divine.
And when the pattern's done we'll see
From Heaven up above
The parts we thought were hard to do
God wove with His own love.

Phyllis C. Michael

He Will
See Us Through

No matter if I'm worried,
No matter if I'm blue,
My loving heavenly Father
Will always see me through!

For He doth dwell within me,
Yet makes no harsh demands;
For when I'm feeling weary,
He takes me by the hand!

So let's not be discouraged
When cares come into view;
For God, our heavenly Father,
Will always see us through!

Sancie Earman King

*When cares abound within me,
Your comfort gladdens my soul.*
Psalm 94:19

Window Sightings

I do not need a mountaintop
Or panoramic view
To know the glory of the Lord,
His love and greatness, too.

I do not need a wide expanse
Of sea and sky so fair...
A single star can light my soul
With joy beyond compare.

A sunbeam dancing on a pane
And moonlight in a tree
Are quite enough to show His face
And bring the Lord to me.

Amy C. Ellis

God Bless the Children

God bless the children one and all
And lift them up if they should fall.
Grant them grace to grow up strong,
To choose the right and not the wrong.
Nurture them with faith and love
That keeps them close to You above.
Lord keep them safe by night and day
And shield them when they go astray.
Instruct them in the ways of prayer
And keep them always in Your care.
Let them bloom like April flowers
And bless their lives as they bless ours.
Be ever near whene'er they call...
God bless the children one and all!

Clay Harrison

*...Great and wonderful are Your
works, Lord God Almighty. Just
and true are Your ways...*
Revelation 15:3

An Autumn Tapestry

I'd like to weave a tapestry
Of rich October's artistry.
I'd gather multicolored leaves
Before they sail on Autumn's breeze.
I'd duplicate with patterns bold
Fall trees the season turns to gold.
I'd stitch with strands of meadow green
That glow like shimmered velveteen.
I'd sew with hues of scarlet thread
The sunset in its fiery bed.
And then my tapestry I'd frame
In Autumn's falling leaves of flame.

Nora M. Bozeman

Autumn Assurance

October unveils her annual display
Under remarkably blue skies each day.
Across hills and dales, panoramas unfold.
Sunlit trees are aflame in scarlet and gold.
Split-rail fences are draped in berries that shine
Like glittering jewels on each twining vine.
Wide fields are laden with pumpkins that glow
Making mouths water for pies we love so.
Vivid Autumn foliage in the lake reflected
Is a visual blessing quite unexpected.
In perfect formation, geese honk in flight.
A giant harvest moon hangs low each night.
Soon November will put Autumn to bed,
And icy Winter will rush in instead.
Giving glorious assurance, God tucks in earth
With a warm, vibrant promise of springtime rebirth!

Louise Pugh Corder

Changing Scenes

August days have left us now.
Autumn drifts on cooler breeze.
Mother Nature's fast at work
Splashing colors on the trees.

Dreamy-eyed September brings
Balmy, lazy, hazy days.
Blue mist veils the distant hills,
September's fair, but brief her stay.

Bright October's just offstage
Ready, waiting for her cue.
Dressed in gold and crimson lace,
All heads turn for her debut.

Look! October's on the hill,
Gold cape swirling in the breeze.
Dancing in red slippers fair
Her debut is sure to please.

We watch spellbound as she paints
Multihues on trees and hills.
Vivid shades come into sight –
Lavishly her gold she spills.

Sun shines down enhancing all.
Proud she is of work she's done.
We rejoice that we have seen
A preview of days to come.

Beverly J. Anderson

God's Wonders

God can do such wondrous things,
He tints the sky so blue,
Paints the robin's breast in Spring,
Designs each season's view.
God puts the song in sparrows,
He scents the lilacs fair,
Gives us the earth's rich bounty,
Makes rosy Autumn's pear.
God sends the rain for harvest,
He warms us with the sun,
And gives us peaceful evening
For rest when day is done.
God blesses with the woodlands,
He layers hills with green,
Make the daisies dance in fields,
Creates most dazzling scenes.
God can do such wondrous things
And greatest of them all,
He gives His love to comfort
If we but seek and call.

Virginia Borman Grimmer

God's Golden Autumn Treasures

Autumn once again is blazing
With its colors bright and bold,
A time of joy and laughter –
Treasures of pure gold.

Fields are abundant with the harvest
Of pumpkins orange and round,
Cobs of corn have fallen
Upon the leafy ground.

The harvest moon is beaming
As hooting owls gather near the barn,
Pheasants and turkeys strut their stuff,
Displaying all their charm.

A dreamy breeze of Autumn
Blows gently on the face
While the leaves of oaks and maples
Tiptoe about the land with grace.
Only God could have created
Such a glorious sight –
From goldenrod to ginkgo's fan
And geese which now take flight.

Linda C. Grazulis

Autumn Blessings

See the goodness of our Father
In the Autumn season fair,
In the colors that delight us
When there's beauty everywhere.

In the gold and crimson hillsides,
In each maple tree ablaze,
In bright goldenrod and asters
Lining rustic country ways.

See the goodness of our Father
In the sky of sapphire-blue,
In the Autumn sun enhancing
Every lovely thing in view.

See the goodness of our Father
In the beauty of the land,
In the lavish yield we gather,
All provided by His hand.

See the goodness of our Father
In the Autumn season fair;
For this wealth of Autumn blessings,
We lift thankful hearts in prayer.

Beverly J. Anderson

Strengthen Me, Lord

Strengthen me, Lord, this I pray,
Guide me through another day.
Clear the darkness of this hour
With Your loving, caring power.

Cleanse my mind of all its fear,
Command them, Lord, to disappear.
Grant me the grace to see things through,
For all my blessings came from You.

Elaine R. Angier

Know That God Is Beside You

See the mountains or the valleys,
See a beautiful plain,
Know that God is beside you,
Be there pleasure or pain.

Watch the sunrise or sunset,
See a field full of grain,
Know that God is beside you
In the sunshine or rain.

Climb the heights of success,
Reach the depths of despair,
Be your heart filled with gladness,
Be it burdened by care.

Reach out to our Father,
Be there loss or gain,
Know that God is beside you,
And there He will remain.

Eleanor M. Torchia

His Tender Love

I cannot fathom days
Without God's tender love,
As deep as any ocean,
As vast as skies above.

He leads me to still waters
And there He sits with me,
He paints for me a vision
That others may not see.

I see Him on the mountains,
In valleys down below,
In every star that shines,
In all of moonlight's glow.

I see Him in each flower
That grows in gardens fair.
He puts a rainbow in the sky
To let me know He's there.

Without a word that's spoken,
He knows my every need,
But having Him so close to me
Is His most wondrous deed.

Edna Fontaine

May the Lord give strength to
His people; may the Lord bless
His people with peace!
Psalm 29:11

Some Small Way

If I can bring a ray of sunshine
Into someone's life today;
If I can, in some small way,
Help chase all their blues away;
If I can say a simple prayer
That will encourage an aching heart,
Then I will feel in some small way
That I have done my part.

Helen Ruth Ashton

The Silent Days

Winter brings the silent days
While on the ground the white snow lays,
All nature lends a quiet real
In peaceful moments quite ideal,
Asleep within the frozen ground,
Each little bulb so safe and sound.

The silent days when home is best,
The special time of gentle rest,
When families gather 'round the fire
To satisfy a heart's desire,
'Tis then our Summer dreams come true,
A happiness for me and you.

We marvel at the magic bliss
We find within a snowflake's kiss,
We meditate on seasons past,
The lovely Fall that couldn't last,
Our faith renewed in many ways
As we delight to silent days.

Garnett Ann Schultz

As long as the earth lasts,
seedtime and harvest, cold and heat,
Summer and Winter, and day and
night shall not cease.
Genesis 8:22

Winter Ballet

I sit here by my window seat
And watch the snowflakes as they fall.
They cover trees in ermine wrap,
And for the shrubs purl lacy shawls.

They swirl right past my windowpane –
White ballerinas twirling 'round.
They dance so gaily through the air,
Merrily whirling, as if wound.

My heart delights in their ballet
Performed with beauty and with grace.
Last dance completed, now they fall,
   The barren earth soon to replace.

All through the night the snowflakes fall.
When dawns the early morning light
   We see a fluffy comforter
Has blanketed the ground in white.

Beverly J. Anderson

Springtime Robins

Spring's glowing enchantment has begun,
Fresh buds and blossoms nod in the sun,
Early robins trill rich songs of praise
In sparkling, spinning roundelays.
Jeweled robins attired in ruby vests,
Within tall oaks, build family nests.
Ambassadors of symphonic song,
A joyous welcome to your vibrant throng.
Flitting high above broad fields of clover,
Greeting fragrant flowers as they fly over,
Friendly robins flutter over the greening sod,
Crowning gift from the graciousness of God.

Elisabeth Weaver Winstead

Heartfelt Words of Praise

How often we call out His name
When we are in distress,
And seek sweet consolation
In His divine caress.

How many times we turn to Him
To lead us on our way
To goals and aspirations
That sometimes go astray.

He shows His tender mercy
When there seems no end in sight
To trials and tribulations –
He becomes our guiding light.

He smiles when we remember
To show we truly care
By saying a fervent "Thank You"
When we speak to Him in prayer.

Catherine Janssen Irwin

When Winter Turns to Spring

Just when the world grows weary
Of Winter's ice and snow,
God sends the lovely springtime
To set our hearts aglow.

Robins come from southern clime
To fill our days with song;
Grass is sprouting fresh and green,
Making beautiful each lawn.

Azaleas and pink dogwoods
Are gloriously abloom,
Dew-drenched lilacs brought indoors
Send forth their sweet perfume.

Crocuses and daffodils,
Tulips in bright array
Now nod for our attention
Along the hill and way.

And I am truly thankful
That Winter's lost its sting
And God in lavish fashion
Is showing off His Spring.

Kay Hoffman

Jesus, I Feel Your Peace

How sweet the world just before dawn,
Before the sun rises out of the sea,
When the flowers shine with morning dew
And birds awake in the tree.

And the peace I feel standing here,
Which only Jesus can truly know,
Will abide with me every hour
Until God bids this day to go.

Virginia Luers

Born Anew

When the month of May begins to fill
The world with multicolored thrills,
And blossoms spring from tiny shoots
While orchards form their luscious fruits –
I see the power of God unfold
Like the closed bud of a fragrant rose.
The dancing of the clover blooms
Fills the earth with sweet perfume.
The earth, reborn anew it seems,
Shakes off my old, idle dreams.
And I, like earth, am born anew
When springtime, again, struts into view!

Barbara Cagle Ray

*You have been born anew, not from
perishable but from imperishable seed,
through the living and abiding
word of God...*
1 Peter 1:23

Summertime

Summertime is all dressed out
In the latest style,
Roses make a grand debut,
Flowers growing wild.

All along a country road,
Daisies take a nod,
Seeds are planted in a field
By the hand of God.

I'm as sure as I can be
That He must have planned,
Angels with their color brush
Paint the flowers grand.

Tiny, little buttercup
In a bright array,
Angels must have painted you
On a sunny day.

Katherine Smith Matheney

August Song

Oh, Summer, do stay longer,
A little longer please –
I still am not quite able
To part with scented breeze
Or say goodbye to hollyhocks
Or droning bumblebees,
Bright butterflies with amber wings
Or hammocks tied to trees.
A chill is in the air now,
I feel Fall drawing near –
Oh, Summer, do not leave us,
Don't go away this year…

Bea Lotz

Listening to the Quiet...

When listening to the quiet,
My God and I commune...
I listen as He whispers,
But I must stay in tune.
He speaks to me through nature
For He created all...
I feel the gentle breezes
And hear the songbird's call.
Listen!...Hear the little bird
Now calling for its mate...
Only God could plan it so
And then, indeed, create.
Stress and fear are pushed aside
For quiet times must be
Times when God alone must have
The top priority.
He whispers gently to me
About His loving care...
"For the lilies of the field
and the birds up in the air.
How much more I'll care for you"
...His special words to me...
If I couldn't hear the quiet,
I'd miss so much, you see.
Lord, keep me always tender
And sensitive to You...
What I hear in the quiet
Restores my faith anew.

Anna M. Matthews

My Little Corner

I have a little corner,
So dear it is to me;
A place that reaches Heaven
Where my Savior's face I see.

It isn't much to look at,
It may be dark and still,
But when I go on bended knee
To know my Father's will,

The darkness seems to fade away,
And sunlight takes its place;
For there is light and glory
Just to look upon His face.

I tell Him how I love Him,
He knows my every care.
If words I cannot find to say,
He sees me kneeling there.

And of all earth's lovely places,
There is none that can compare
To that secret little corner
Where I meet my Lord in prayer.

Helen Humbarger

The Earth Sings Forth...

The earth sings forth God's glory
With merriment and praise,
And all the creatures great and small
To Him their voices raise.

The birds carol with melody
To worship before His throne,
For no other deserves such glory
But God and God alone.

Flowers bedecked in colors bright
Bow with awesome hue,
Thanking Him for robes so rich,
For rain and sunshine, too.

Streams chant in rhythmic tones,
Rivers overflow their banks,
For earth's realms can never be enough
To proclaim the endless thanks.

The earth sings forth a melody
Of thanksgiving and prayer,
And we as chosen men of God
Reflect His image here.

Janice George

*Therefore will I proclaim You, O Lord,
among the nations, and I will sing
praise to Your name.*
Psalm 18:50

Lord, Lead Me

Lord, take away the distractions
That creep into my day.
Lead me, gently lead me
Along Your perfect way.

Put blinders on my eyes
That I look straight ahead,
Not at the world –
With all its fear and dread.

I know that I may stumble,
But You are there to guide –
I know without a doubt, my Lord,
You're always at my side.

Dona M. Maroney

Footsteps by the Seashore

The sea in her loneliness
Rushes onto the shore;
Earth and ocean merge briefly –
A second, no more!

I stand by the seaside,
Footprints in the sand
Which the ocean erases
With a sweep of her hand!

I gaze over the waters
So majestically crowned
With billowing whitecaps
And great roaring sound!

My soul is enraptured,
Yet lonely I stand –
Footprints by the seashore
Swept away from the sand!

Elizabeth B. Delea

The Last Days of Summer

During the last days of Summer
When the earth is dry and still,
Wind blows the first fallen leaves
Across the wooded hills.

The rose that brought such pleasure
Now bids a fond farewell
As it sheds its velvety petals
Across the grassy dell.

I must say goodbye to Summer skies
And to fields of goldenrods,
And to daffodils that line the hills
With their slow and gentle nods.

Seasons come and seasons go
And I know that Summer must surrender
To the beauty of the Autumn
That fills the earth with splendor.

Shirley Hile Powell

I'm Always
Chasing Rainbows

I'm always chasing rainbows
Or wishing on a star.
I love the things of Nature
That beckon from afar.

I love to watch a hummingbird
Fly backwards from the vine,
And frosted leaves in Autumn
Simply are divine.

A sunset at the seaside
Sets my heart aflame,
For every one's a masterpiece
And no two are the same.

I'm always chasing rainbows,
Building castles in the air,
For the majesty of Nature
Confirms that God's still there.

Clay Harrison

Autumn

The scenic beauty of Autumn
Is something to behold
In her regal garment
Of orange, reds and gold.

Her robe made by the Master,
Each leaf touched by His hand,
Making Summer's exit
So royal and so grand.

Autumn makes us look upward,
For maybe we will see
Beyond this miracle of beauty
The One who makes it be.

Josephine Anne Miller

Fall Is in the Air

A tinge of Fall is in the air;
Its pungent scent I smell,
Cool sunset hues wash o'er the land
To cast an eerie spell.

The somber clouds of steely gray
Cast shadows by my chair;
Outside my window, leaves waltz by –
Yes, Fall is in the air.

When Autumn fires the distant hills
And sets the woods ablaze
With colors that no man can match,
I must give God the praise!

For it was He who made it all –
The earth, the sky, the sea,
The animals, the plants and man,
And He loves you and me.

He loved so much, He came and died
And paid the price of sin
That you and I, if we believe,
Can dwell fore'er with Him!

Luther Elvis Albright

I Shall Not Want

No need have I which God does not see,
My path to Him is clear.
I shall not fear in darkness or light,
I know my Lord is near.

No pain have I which God does not know,
My comfort still is He;
In joy or woe out of the depths,
His peace shall come to me.

No cry escapes the ears of my Lord,
He hears each humble plea,
And day by day, His love shall provide
All that is best for me.

Phyllis C. Michael

My Overseer and Guide

I'm always so glad my Savior is with me
As awakening sun embraces dawn,
Then quickly swallows the darkness up
'Til each of the shining stars is gone!

And glad that He leads throughout the day
On familiar paths or paths unknown –
Though I journey near or journey far
Or quiet abide within my home.

With grace and mercy, Jesus guides –
Guides through the joys or the trials of each day:
Carries burdens, eases my load,
Overshadows the darkness, lightens my way!

Always He's opened the pathways before me –
Thus Jesus, my Savior, holds my heart's key;
So I know I can trust the future to Him,
For all of my days He will oversee!

Lynn Fenimore Nuzzi

He refreshes my soul.
He guides me in right paths for
His name's sake.
Psalm 23:3

Autumntime

Oh, how I love the autumntime
When God sets the earth aflame.
Trees look like golden pillars
Lining our little country lane.

Scarlet leaves have a fiery glow
That makes me almost breathless.
Frost scattered throughout the fields
Tends to make me kind of restless.

I love to carve the pumpkin
With a mighty scary face
And taste the sweet, juicy apples
Over by the old home place.

The creek bed is nearly dry
And the barn is filled with hay.
The air feels so cool and crisp
On an Indian Summer's day.

When Autumn gives way to Winter,
I'll feel sad to see her part.
Her memories will remain forever
In the deepest part of my heart.

Shirley Hile Powell

He only is my Rock and my Salvation, my Stronghold; I shall not be disturbed at all.

Psalm 62:3

Never Alone

He can calm the troubled waters
When you walk in dark despair.
There is hope when you feel helpless
Knowing that the Lord is there...

Sharing in your sunshine moments
Or in valleys deep and wide,
He will never, ever leave you –
He is always by your side.

There's no other friend so faithful
Through the sunshine and the rain,
Through the teardrops and the laughter,
In your joy and in your pain.

We could never, ever thank Him
For His love He gives so free,
Never changing... never ending
Throughout all eternity.

Oh, the wonder of all wonders
As we live from day to day
Knowing that we have a Father
Who is with us all the way.

Gertrude B. McClain

When Winter Comes!

When Winter visits us at last
With many an icy, chilling blast,
And scatters mounds of fallen leaves
Until they hide in shrubs and eaves,
We mourn the gentler seasons past!

When snow comes down for many days
And hills are cloaked in silver haze;
When all the ground is frozen hard
And slippery slopes put us on guard,
We rail at Winter's devious ways!

And yet, when Winter brings, as well,
A log fire's own delightful smell;
The rosy cheeks on each small face
As children play outside our place
And snowballs fly and "targets" yell.

We find that Winter's not so bad,
But offers much to make us glad:
Fond memories of holidays
With loved ones shared in many ways
That once, in wintertime, we had!

John C. Bonser

God's Blessings

God sends His light to shine on us
And brighten up our day.
He guides us with a steady hand
So we won't lose our way.

God gives us strength to face our ills
And teaches us to cope.
He never burdens us with things
Which lie beyond our scope.

He blesses us with happiness
And bestows His loving peace
And makes our life a pleasant place
Where ills will find release.

Dolores Karides

Bits of Joy

God blesses us with bits of joy
Like flowers strewn our way
To give us strength and courage
So we can cope with each new day.

That's why we have the sunshine
After darkness and the rain,
And why we are given laughter
To help ease our sorrow and pain.

The wonders of nature around us,
All those who share our love,
And work worth more than riches
Are bits of joy sent from above.

Eva Marie Ippolito

Winter Nighttime Wonder

Oh, Winter nighttime wonder
When the earth is calm and still.
I watch in peaceful moments
Snowflakes landing on windowsill.

The darkened night is soon made bright
As the moon through clouds appears,
And makes ghostlike shadows
In the wintertime of the year.

The earth is white and glistens
With the fresh, white fallen snow.
Icicles found on the roof's edge
Appear likes prisms hanging below.

Thank You, Lord, for the wintertime
That allows us to slow down
And take in all of its splendor
With the beauty that abounds.

Shirley Hile Powell

Spring Beauties

Spring beauties carpet woodland floors
And dance upon the Maytime moors.
Each pretty, little blossom blue,
Does tell us Spring has come anew.

They quite enchant, so comely shy,
As close to earth they lovely lie.
Spring beauties have a charm apart
To warm a Winter-weary heart!

Virginia Borman Grimmer

Throughout the Day

When the early dawn bids adieu
To the gently fading night,
And the flowers lift their faces
To softly kiss the light,
'Tis then, within your chamber 'lone,
Your heart should plant such seeds
That through the day will manifest
As good and loving deeds.

Then, as the fleeting hours pass
And the turmoil of the day
Envelops 'round you like a cloud
To block your chosen way,
'Tis then, within your inner heart,
This question should arise:
"Am I trying, striving, living,
As I would before His eyes?"

When the day is done and ended
And the world is hushed in sleep,
And over all the moon and stars
Their silent vigil keep,
'Tis then that you should be prepared
To pass the Spirit's test –
Ah, what sweet joy to rest in Him,
Knowing you've done your best.

Esther Nilsson

Each Spring Is New

We still have the tulips,
The skies soft and blue,
The green grass of splendor
And daffodils too,
The birdsong – the nesting
And buds bursting forth,
The magic of lilacs,
The joy of rebirth.

Each soft April shower
That falls from the sky,
The so-gentle breezes
That whisper and sigh,
Perfume from the blossoms,
Each leaf of bright green,
The sun and the shadows
That glisten and gleam.

We've known all these pleasures
From years long ago,
The wonders of April
And Maytime aglow,
Each miracle treasured,
Green grass kissed with dew,
Though so oft repeated,
Yet each Spring is new.

Garnett Ann Schultz

Splendor and majesty go before Him;
praise and joy are in His holy place.
1 Chronicles 16:27

Gratitude

I thank You, Lord, for all the gifts
You've given me today.
For all the friends that smile at me
And the kindly things they say.

I thank You for the helping hand
My friends have given me.
I thank You for the kind pretense
That my faults they did not see.

I thank You for the blessings
That You give our happy land;
I know that all that comes our way
Is brought here by Your hand.

Rev. Thomas Foy

My Riches

I sense the warming touch of sun,
Behold each shining ray,
Watch opal clouds go drifting by,
And I feel rich today.

I listen to a bluebird sing,
A melody to play,
And gather flowers in a field,
Oh, I feel rich today.

I see ripe fruit upon a tree,
Hear sheep in gentle bay,
Watch golden butterflies waft by,
Oh, I feel rich today.

A myriad of precious things
Do all around me lay.
Great bounty in my treasure chest,
Oh, I feel rich today!

Virginia Borman Grimmer

On a Golden Summer's Day

Summer's beauty is abounding
From the labors of the Spring.
Flowers in bloom are breathtaking.
What color and fragrance they bring!

Lush, green fields are mingled
With small, bright, golden manes,
Which seem to sway in gentle breeze
And set the earth aflame.

The menagerie of flighty birds
Orchestrate their melodious song.
They fill me with joy and elation
And a peace for which I long.

A gift from God, the Summer sky,
Colored with the brightest blue;
And then appears white, fluffy clouds,
"Like ships sailing through."

I'll be content with trickling streams
And music that rivers play.
My senses are filled with pure delight
All on a golden Summer's day.

Shirley Hile Powell

Fill us at daybreak with Your kindness,
that we may shout for joy and
gladness all of our days.
Psalm 90:14

Make a Joyful Noise

Make a joyful noise unto the Lord,
Sing praises to His most precious name.
O, lift up high your voices
And His mighty words proclaim.

Go and tell the old, old story,
Go tell of Jesus and His love.
He's the Prince of peace and glory.
He's our gift from Heaven above.

Jesus gave His life for you and me.
Sing out and let every voice reveal
Through Him there is salvation
And His tender love is real.

Let the streams of living waters
Keep flowing as you sing your song.
Make a joyful noise unto the Lord,
For to Him you do belong.

John and Edna Massimilla

Bridges
of Understanding

Bridges of understanding
Erected of God-given strength,
The power to trust in a Spirit,
The passion to go the length.

Bridges of understanding
Crossing the depths of my soul,
Spanning those ill-fated waters,
Desperate to find my goal.

Bridges of understanding
Linking this Heaven and earth,
Therein, the coveted treasure,
Therein, the key to rebirth.

Janice Cortis

But it is a spirit in man, the
breath of the Almighty, that gives
him understanding.
Job 32:8

Those Hazy Days
of Summer

Oh, those hazy days of Summer –
Just musing where I lie
To see ships of clouds go sailing
Through the cerulean Summer sky.

My thoughts go sailing with the clouds
Above the earth so high,
Far away from bustling crowds
Just watching time pass by.

Yes, I can hear the crickets quit
And the droning of the bee.
The noisy, little, twittering wren
Is very close to me.

Still my thoughts are far away
Drifting with the breeze,
Making a pleasant roundelay
Of a land beyond the seas.

A land where golden streets arise
Beyond the walls of jasper.
With pearled gates that open wide
To welcome home a traveler.

Ruth J. Tabberer

God Is Everything I Need

God has my hand and walks with me.
He is my eyes so I may see.
He is my ears so I may hear.
He is the strength that holds me near.
Each day He simply shows the way
To walk beside Him every day.
He is my friend, He is my guide.
My empty spirit He will hide.
He knows each breath before I speak.
He heals my body when I'm weak.
He gives me love and comforts me.
When evening comes, He sets me free,
A greater master cannot be.
Yes, Lord, my God, I'll walk with Thee.

Edna Louise Gilbert

A Rose

The rose is such a tender plant
And needs much loving care,
With this 'twill grow in simple soil
And flourish anywhere.

A rose is such a perfect flower,
God sent His gentle touch
To brighten up a lonely spot
For one we love so much.

Our life is like a little rose,
We see it bloom and fall.
He made our life, He made a rose,
The most perfect gifts of all.

Maxine Lyga

Let justice descend, O heavens, like dew from
above, like gentle rain let the skies drop it
down. Let the earth open and salvation
bud forth; let justice also spring up!
I, the Lord, have created this.
Isaiah 45:8

For All Tomorrows

He's the glistening frost come daybreak,
The azure of the sky,
The colors in the leaves of Fall,
An eagle's searching eye.

He's the crashing waves of oceans,
A violet's subtle hue,
The birds that sing in springtime bliss,
An evening's diamond dew.

He's the Winter's lacy snowflakes,
The sunlight's warming rays,
The fragrance of a Summer rose,
A little child who plays.

He's the rhyme on tongues of poets,
The winds within a sail,
The wobbly legs of newborn fawn,
The ringing of a bell.

He's the hope for all tomorrows,
The answer to each prayer,
He's the Lord of vast dominions –
I sense Him everywhere.

Henry W. Gurley

Have You?

Have you seen an oak tree
In an acorn on the ground,
Or heard a glorious anthem
In a baby's cooing sound?

Have you seen your Mom
In a piece of pumpkin pie,
Or caught a glimpse of God
In a starry, moonlit sky?

Have you seen an angel
In a snowflake on the walk,
Or had a glimpse of Heaven
As you watch a soaring hawk?

To experience the joy and wonders
In visions such as these,
I give grateful thanks to God
And fall upon my knees!

Mildred Hechler

His Blessings
All Around Us

Thank Him for the little things
That happen every day –
The bird songs at your window,
Or a little squirrel at play…

The laughter of a little child
That warms the coldest heart,
A sweet sunset at evening
As another day departs.

Yes, thank Him for the little things
That happen by the hour.
Give glory to almighty God
And His creative power.

Mary Ann Jameson

*When you hearken to the voice of the
Lord, your God, all these blessings will
come upon you and overwhelm you.*
Deuteronomy 28:2

The Voice of God

God speaks to us in many ways.
Whene'er we listen, we will hear
His voice in every leaf that rustles,
Whispering that He is near.

His love sounds in the newborn's cry
And in the morning call of doves;
The brook that ripples, splashing by,
And in the voice of those we love.

He is a patient, caring Father,
Heeding not the winds that sigh
As they betray with tales of weakness.
He forgives, if we but try.

God will show us His compassion,
Loving us, though things go wrong.
He is there for us to turn to.
Hear the hope in each bird song!

Who could despair when through our day
God reaffirms so many ways
That He is with us? Hear His message.
Join all nature! Sing His praise!

Helen M. Motti

God Is Everywhere

He's the smile on a face…
A note in the mail,
The breeze on the ocean
That propels a sail.
Food in the pantry…
Wood on the fire,
Shoes on our feet…
Words that inspire.
Let's not get so busy
That we miss all His signs…
They're His way of blessing
Both your days and mine.

Frances Gregory Pasch

Comfort

When sorrow lays its heavy hand
Upon our lives and hearts,
We stand in need of loving words,
The hope that faith imparts;
Of holding close dear memories
And knowing God does send
The strength to do the things we must
And slowly, too, to mend.
Yet most, we need to know the truth,
That God is at our side
And since our loved ones do,
We know, now with God abide,
Then, as is our blessed Lord,
They're just a prayer away.
May this truth, like sun through clouds,
Give peace to you today.

Minnie Boyd Popish

When cares abound within me,
Your comfort gladdens my soul.
Psalm 94:19

At Harvest Time

Surely the Lord showeth mercy
Unto the children of earth,
For the crops have grown aplenty
Since the first Spring buds took birth.

The gardens lie ripe in the sun,
The corn in the fields stands tall,
The small grain is stored in the bins,
And man need not dread the Fall.

No hail, nor wind, nor storm has come
To halt the growth of the seed,
Or raging waters yet consumed
The fruit of the planter's deed.

No frost has harmed the tender ears
Or stolen the flowers' gold,
Another year of bumper crops
From our countryside is told.

Oh, surely these gifts from the Lord
Are more than the heart can praise,
Enough to meet our hungry need
From the rich, black soil we raise.

Edna Pinkerton Hirons

A Prayer

Dear God in Heaven, give me faith
To always trust in You,
To help me through life's problems
Be they many or be they few.

Draw me closer, God, to Thee,
This is my daily prayer,
And when I err, dear God, forgive,
Help me know You're always there…

To ease my every burden,
To lighten every load,
If I follow in Your footsteps
As I travel down life's road.

Maryalice Friday

Trust

I do believe Your promises;
I've found them always true.
I know the gladness of my heart
Does ever come from You.
I know my prayers are answered,
Yet, sometimes, I know delay,
Wherein You teach me patience and
Desire to trust Your way.
Forgive the moments of despair
That grow as I protest
The things that do not go my way,
Forgetting You know best.
Help me resolve to just accept
Your sovereign will for me
To keep, in perfect peace, my heart,
My mind steadfast on Thee.

Anna Lee Edwards McAlpin

Love, Perfect Love

Oh, love, love, perfect love
That makes my heart take wing.
Release your power
And let me soar,
Oh, how my soul does sing!

It sings of praises
Meant for Thee,
Of thankfulness and love,
For all things in
This whole wide earth
Created from above.

The morning sun
So bright and clear,
The noonday's gentle breeze,
The evening sunset,
Pink and gold,
That brings its restful ease.

I praise the Lord
For all of life,
Whatever it may be.
Regardless of
Our outward look,
He dwells in
You and me.

He loves us,
Each and every one,
Whether near or far,
And lets us know
That love's for us,
No matter who we are.

Marceine Melcher

Your love is before my eyes; I walk
guided by Your faithfulness.
Psalm 26:3

The Snow

It sifted down upon the ground,
It drifted 'neath the trees,
It sat upon the fence post round,
It shifted with the breeze.
It filled the air with flecks of white,
The paths and roads impearled.
Oh, great delight! This fluff last night
Transformed the whole wide world.

Ruth J. Tabberer

When There Is Love

With love in your heart,
You can't ever go wrong;
You'll welcome each day
With a smile or a song.

You can look to your heart
When it's guidance you need,
Never finding a trace
Of malice or greed.

Each challenge you'll meet,
You will see as a test
To prove to the world
It can bring out your best.

With love in your heart,
You'll be certain to find
The end of the rainbow
And sweet peace of mind.

Catherine Janssen Irwin

A Moment in Time

The landscape has been frozen
For a moment in time
For Winter worked her magic
In a moment so sublime.

While the weary world was sleeping,
God covered it with snow,
With purple shadows creeping
To the villages below.

In the solitude of starlight,
Earth became a wonderland
Of frosted leaves and pumpkins
Wrought by the Master's hand.

Earth seemed newly created
In the twinkling of an eye,
And I know that God was smiling
Somewhere in the sky.

Clay Harrison.